Marsha Ottum Owen

UNCLE CARL HAS A CHICKEN ON HIS HEAD!

Thanks to R.K. and the rest of my family and friends who have encouraged me.
Great thanks to my writing critique group-Simona, Danette, Noemie, and Dulcie. You're the best!
And a special thanks also to designer, Tom Barrett, who put in much effort to make it look
so much better than I ever could have on my own!

In memory of my Uncle Carl-who really DID have a chicken on his head!

Copyright © 2019 by Marsha Ottum Owen.
All rights reserved.

Designed by Tom Barrett.

ISBN: 978-0-9976275-1-0

UNCLE CARL...

...has a chicken on his head!
A chicken on his head?
Yes, a chicken on his head!

It's sitting there picking at a long piece of thread.

Uncle Carl has a chicken on his neck!
A chicken on his neck?
Yes, a chicken on his neck!
That chicken truly loves him.
It just gave him a peck.

Uncle Carl has a chicken on his hand!
A chicken on his hand?
Yes, a chicken on his hand!
It's having fun
　　plucking on
　　　a blue
　　　　rubber band.

Uncle Carl has a chicken on his belly!
   A chicken on his belly?
Yes, a chicken on his belly!
I can't tell you why,
   but that chicken sure is smelly!

Uncle Carl has a chicken on his arm!
A chicken on his arm?
Yes, a chicken on his arm!

That clever little chicken
 wants to freshen up the farm!

Uncle Carl has a chicken on his hip!
 A chicken on his hip?
Yes, a chicken on his hip!
It better hold on tight or
 that chicken's going to slip!

Uncle Carl has a chicken on his leg!
 A chicken on his leg?
Yes, a chicken on his leg!
It's fat, and it's wiggling
 like it's going to lay an egg!

Uncle Carl has a chicken on his knee.
A chicken on his knee?
Yes, a chicken on his knee!
It's sitting there sipping on
a cup of herbal tea.

Uncle Carl has a chicken on his shin!
   A chicken on his shin?
Yes, a chicken on his shin!
That poor scraggly chicken
   is only bones and skin!

Uncle Carl has a chicken on his toe!
 A chicken on his toe?
Yes, a chicken on his toe!
I'd say that last chicken
 doesn't know where else to go!

Uncle Carl has ten chickens
on him now!
Ten chickens on him now?
Yes, ten chickens on him now!
Well... that's all the chickens.....

BUT...

UH OH!

HERE COMES THE COW!!

THE REAL UNCLE CARL
(WITH A CHICKEN ON HIS HEAD)

One day my cousin posted a faded picture of my Uncle Carl on Facebook. He was sitting on the ground with a chicken on his head and a grin on his face. I laughed. When I asked her if there was a story behind that photo, she said she didn't know of one. That picture stuck in my head and one day, a rhyme came to my mind! I wrote it down and decided to attempt to make it into a book. After a lot of trial and error and help from other creatives, this book is the result. My hope is that many little people will enjoy this book, as well as my Ottum kin who remember Uncle Carl Ottum with love and fondness.

MARSHA OTTUM OWEN

Marsha lives with her husband, R.K., in a fifth wheel. As full-time RVers, they enjoy traveling and pursuing their passions while trying to follow the sun (though it doesn't always cooperate). Marsha's goal is to illustrate, and sometimes write, 10 picture books before she leaves this earth. *Uncle Carl Has a Chicken on His Head* is number three. Two more are in the works. She, along with her art, is ever a work in progress! You can follow her progress on her facebook page: Marsha Ottum Owen Books.

Made in the USA
Middletown, DE
06 December 2023

44674679R00020